PALESTINE A - Z

KATE THOMPSON

LIMINAL
BOOKS

ISBN (paperback) 978-1-913544-20-1
ISBN (ebook) 978-1-913544-21-8

Introduction

'IT'S COMPLICATED!'

Palestine A - Z is intended to contradict this claim, which we hear too often in relation to the Israeli occupation of Palestine. It isn't complicated at all, but there are a lot of key elements which, for those who are interested in the issue, it is helpful to understand.

This is not a history. There are plenty of those available and a reading and resources list has been added at the end for anyone who wants to explore further.

The entries draw upon a wide range of sources, including Palestinian, Israeli, British, American and international. Everything is in alphabetical order. Items in the text which have their own entry are marked with an asterisk (*).

The Abraham Accords
See Normalisation*

Administrative Detention

Administrative detention refers to the arrest and detention of individuals by a state without trial on alleged security grounds, and is applied by Israel in the occupied Palestinian Territories. Under the terms of the 1979 Emergency Powers, detainees can be held indefinitely without charge or trial if it is suspected that they may commit a crime in the future. This form of arrest and detention operates alongside a dual legal system in the West Bank, under which Palestinians are prosecuted in military courts, while Israeli settlers are prosecuted in civilian courts, with greater rights and protections. Palestinian children are the only children in the world to be systematically prosecuted in military courts.

Administrative detention has been widely criticised by international human rights organisations for bypassing regular judicial processes, indefinite imprisonment, reliance on secret classified evidence or no evidence, and mistreatment of detainees, but Israel justifies its use as a preventative measure. Between October 2023 and June 2024 there were 7,170 administrative detention orders.

'Administrative detention is based on secret suspicions, secret evidence and no charges being brought. To conceal its inherent absurdity, hearings are held in-camera and away from the public eye. As such, even the little that is revealed to the defence remains prohibited for publication'. - Haaretz May 2024

AIPAC

The American Israel Public Affairs Committee is a powerful pro-Israel lobby group. *'We are more than 3 million pro-Israel Americans from every congressional district who are working to strengthen bipartisan support for the U.S.-Israel relationship.'* - (AIPAC website)

AIPAC seeks to promote pro-Israel election candidates and defeat those who are critical of Israel's policies. In the 2022 US elections, AIPAC spent $17.5m on supporting pro-Israel candidates. 98% of those they supported won their seats. In 2024 it spent $14.5m on unseating one candidate, Jamaal Bowman, in New York.

'Democrats and Republicans alike fear the lobby's clout. They all know that any politician who challenges its policies stands little chance of becoming president.' - John Mearsheimer and Stephen Wall, *The Israel Lobby and US Foreign Policy*, 2007

AIPAC has also funded MPs in the UK, alongside the British lobby groups Conservative Friends of Israel (CFI) and Labour Friends of Israel (LFI). (Declassified UK).

Anti-Semitism

Anti-Semitism is a form of racism aimed specifically at Jewish people. It is a largely European phenomenon, and has led to periodic assaults on Jewish communities throughout history. The worst of these was in Nazi Germany, which culminated in the death camps and gas chambers responsible for the deaths of 6 million Jews.

In recent times, there is increasing pressure from supporters of Israel to define Israel as 'the collective Jew' and to conflate criticism of Israeli policies and Zionism* with anti-Semitism. Many Jewish people do not subscribe to Zionism and reject these definitions. They view Israel's occupation of Palestine as a driver of anti-Semitism which endangers their security.

*'**Anti-Zionism is not about Jews, it is about Israel.**'*
Avi Shlaim, Israeli-British historian. Al Jazeera May 2024

Apartheid

Apartheid is a system of institutionalised racial segregation and discrimination that originated in South Africa and has been extended in modern usage to describe similar practices elsewhere. Apartheid was codified in the Rome Statute of the International Criminal Court as a crime against humanity, cementing its status as an atrocity crime of the utmost gravity. This regime enforces a strict racial hierarchy, restricting the rights of the oppressed group through legal and extralegal means. In the context of Israel and Palestine, many Palestinian, Israeli and international human rights organisations, including Al-Haq, B'Tselem, Human Rights Watch and Amnesty International, have documented policies that meet the criteria of apartheid, such as the systematic privileging of one ethnic group over another through laws, policies, and practices.

'There is an apartheid state here. In a territory where two people are judged under two legal systems, that is an apartheid state.' - Tamir Pardo, former head of Mossad, September 2023

Arab Jews

Arab Jews are members of the Jewish faith or culture who are ethnically Arab and traditionally spoke Arabic. They were widespread throughout the Arab world before the creation of Israel. Like Arab Christians, they were free to practise their religion subject to certain conditions (e.g. separate tax laws applied), and in all other ways were assimilated into Arab societies. There is still a small Jewish community in Tunisia, but with the rise of Zionism and the creation of the state of Israel, the position of Arab Jews in countries such as Iraq, Yemen, Syria and Lebanon became insecure, and most of them left their homes and settled in Israel.

In the late 19th century there were 24,000 Arab Jews in Palestine, representing around 5% of the population. The First Palestinian Congress of 1919 extended a welcome to those Jews 'among us...who have been living in our province since before the war; they are as we are, and their loyalties are our own.' The PLO* Charter of 1994 stated that 'The Jews who had normally resided in Palestine until the beginning of the Zionist invasion will be considered Palestinians.'

Arab jews were discriminated against by European Ashkanazi jews in Israel. Many of their descendants do not speak Arabic and have no relationship with their countries of origin, but they continue to be under-represented in positions of political power in modern-day Israel.

Balfour Declaration

On November 2nd 1917, Arthur James Balfour, the British Foreign Secretary, issued the following statement, which has become known as the Balfour Declaration.

'His majesty's government view with favour the establishment in Palestine of a national home for the Jewish people and will use their best endeavours to facilitate the achievement of this object, it being clearly understood that nothing shall be done which may prejudice the civil and religious rights of existing non-Jewish communities in Palestine or the rights and political status enjoyed by Jews in any other country.'

The statement gave legitimacy to the Zionist movement growing in Europe, and ultimately led to the establishment of the State of Israel.

BDS (Boycott, Divestment, Sanctions)

The Boycott, Divestment, Sanctions (BDS) movement is a global campaign promoting various forms of boycott against Israel. Launched in 2005 by 170 Palestinian civil society groups,

BDS was inspired by the anti-apartheid movement in South Africa. It seeks to pressure Israel to end its occupation of Palestinian territories, ensure full equality for Arab-Palestinian citizens of Israel, and respect the right of return for Palestinian refugees.

'Boycott' includes calls for Israel's exclusion from cultural and sporting events and from academic institutions, and the rejection of Israeli goods and services by individuals and commercial enterprises.

'Divestment' calls for companies and investment funds to withdraw from existing involvement with Israeli banks and corporate institutions.

'Sanctions' are instruments used by governments which include embargoes on providing weapons and military aid and cessation of trade and diplomatic relations with Israel.

The BDS movement selects targets for campaigns, and has had notable successes in persuading companies to divest from Israeli institutions or change their procurement policies. As of June 2024 they have been less successful in persuading governments to impose sanctions.

BDS has been made illegal in 38 US states. A bill to make it illegal in the UK failed in 2024.

The British Mandate

During WW1, anticipating the demise of the Ottoman Empire, Britain promised the Arab leader Sharif Hussein an Arab kingdom, to include Palestine, in return for help in fighting the Turks. In secret agreements between Britain and France, most of the Ottoman territory was divided into spheres of influence, but the future of Palestine was not decided until 1920, when a League of Nations meeting in Paris agreed on a British Mandate. The mandate incorporated and amplified the Balfour Declaration,* and the promise to Sharif Hussein was reneged upon, creating resentment across the Arab world.

Opposition to their rule in Palestine led the British to take repressive measures against the indigenous population, many of which, such as administrative detention*, collective punishment* and house demolitions were adopted by the Israeli state and are in use to this day. The 1936 uprising, or Great Palestinian Revolt, called for an end to Britain's support for Zionist colonisation and a guarantee of Palestinian self-determination. Britain's subsequent efforts to limit Jewish immigration were met with violent resistance from the Zionist Haganah, Irgun and Stern Gang forces. In 1948 Britain relinquished its mandate and in the same year the State of Israel was proclaimed.

Checkpoints

Large areas of the West Bank and many of its roads are off-limit to Palestinians. In addition, there are upwards of 600 checkpoints and permanent roadblocks, making travel unpredictable and increasing journey times, sometimes by several multiples. Farmers can be separated from their land by checkpoint gates that are often closed and unmanned. Palestinians need permits to enter Jerusalem, and basic entitlements such as hospital appointments are regularly missed because applications for permits are not processed in time.

Temporary checkpoints can appear without notice, and some permanent ones have caged approaches where Palestinians can be detained for hours at the whim of the authorities, giving rise to humiliation as well as frustration. Delays at checkpoints cause schoolchildren to miss lessons or exams and workers to lose employment. There are documented cases of patients dying in cars and ambulances while held up at checkpoints.

Civilian Casualties

See Proportionality

Collective Punishment

Israel has faced numerous accusations of collective punishment of Palestinian civilians, a practice where punitive measures are imposed on a population for actions committed by individuals, or members of a group. This is prohibited by Article 33 of the Fourth Geneva Convention, and violates the fundamental legal principle that the innocent should never be punished for the deeds of others. Arbitrary arrest, raids, and demolition of homes in the occupied Palestinian territories have been highlighted by human rights groups as applications of collective punishment.

In the wake of the Hamas-led October 7th attacks, Israeli forces have used unprecedented force and targeted residential areas, schools, hospitals, and refugee camps, and destroyed essential infrastructure, all while blocking supplies of food, fuel, medical supplies and humanitarian aid, leading to the deaths of more than 37,000 Palestinians, including more than 14,000 children (as of 7th June 2024). All these are examples of extreme collective punishment.

Crimes Against Humanity

Crimes against humanity are grave crimes, committed in peace time or in times of war, which require the existence of a policy to attack a civilian population through the commission of one or more of a list of acts as part of a widespread or systematic attack. Examples are murder, extermination, apartheid,* persecution and other inhuman acts.

Dahiya/Dahieh Doctrine

The Dahiya, or Dahieh doctrine is a tactic adopted by the Israeli military since 2006. It is named for the southern suburb of Beirut: Dahieh, which was destroyed during Israel's war on Lebanon in 2006, using 2000 lb bombs and other heavy ordnance. The strategy was explained in 2008 by major-general Gadi Eisenkot, later Israeli Chief of Staff:

'What happened in the Dahieh quarter will happen in every village from which Israel is fired on. We will apply disproportionate force on it, and cause great damage and destruction there. From our standpoint, these are not civilian villages. They are military bases. This is not a recommendation, this is a plan, and it has been approved.'

Successive assaults on Gaza can be seen as expressions of the Dahieh Doctrine.

Distinction in International Humanitarian Law

The principle of distinction dictates that attacks may only be directed at military objectives and military personnel, not civilians and civilian objects. Indiscriminate attacks are attacks which are not sufficiently clearly directed at a clear military objective and, as such, violate the principle of distinction. Criminal violations of the prohibition on attacking civilians have been included in the application by the ICC's prosecutor for arrest warrants against two Israeli leaders.

Fatah

Fatah is the largest faction of the PLO.* Its leader, Mahmoud Abbas (Abu-Mazen) is one of its founder members and is currently head of the Palestinian Authority.*

Fatah is a secular organisation. The Oslo* talks were made conditional upon Fatah renouncing armed conflict and recognising Israel. It seeks to negotiate the creation of an independent Palestinian state. (See two-state solution*).

Fatah lost the 2006 legislative elections by a wide margin, but following the boycott of Hamas* by Israel and its major backers, Fatah gained control of the PA in the West Bank,* while Hamas took control in Gaza.*

From the River to the Sea

'From the river to the sea, Palestine will be free' is a chant frequently heard at rallies in support of Palestine across the English-speaking world. It was first used by the PLO* in the early 1960s, calling for a single Arab state, but following revisions to its political aspirations, it became a call for a secular democratic state in the region (see one-state solution*). In more recent years it is seen as a demand for recognition of Palestinian rights in the area, with no specific political outcome implied.

A counter-definition used by supporters of Israel claims that 'from the river to the sea' is a call for genocide against the Jewish people, and the use of the phrase has been criminalised in Germany.

Israel's borders with Syria, Lebanon and the OPT* are internationally defined as contested. The Israeli constitution does not define its borders, but in January 2024, Benjamin Netanyahu, speaking in Hebrew, asserted that in any future arrangement, Israel would have to take full control of the entire area 'from the river to the sea.'

> *'(There is) no greater insult to every foundational principle of the United Nations than seeing Netanyahu display before the UNGA a 'map of Israel' that straddles the entire land from the river to the sea, negating Palestine and its people, then attempting to spin the audience with rhetoric about 'peace' in the region, all the while entrenching the longest ongoing belligerent occupation in today's world.'* - Palestinian Ambassador to Germany Laith Arafeh

Gaza

Gauze, used for surgical dressings, takes its name from Gaza, where fine fabrics were woven and traded. Gaza City was a thriving port and centre of commerce in pre-Mandate Palestine.

70% of Palestinians in Gaza are refugees, expelled during the Nakba* and subsequent waves of displacement. Along with the West Bank,* Gaza came under Israeli occupation in 1967. Although Israel built settlements in the strip, they were dismantled in 2005, when Israel changed its policy towards Gaza. When Hamas took over in 2007, Israel imposed a blockade on the entire strip, erecting a fence, and policing the coast. Since that time, nothing and no one has been allowed into or out of Gaza without Israel's permission.

Gaza's economy has atrophied as a result of the blockade. An IMF report in 2022 stated the employment rate to be 45%. Since the Hamas-led attack in October 2023 and the subsequent Israeli assault, unemployment levels have risen to 79% and the GDP has reduced by 83%. (June 2024).

Successive attacks on Gaza since 2009 are designed to damage Hamas' military capabilities and are referred to as 'mowing the grass'.

'Just like mowing your front lawn, this is constant, hard work. If you fail to do so, weeds grow wild and snakes begin to slither around in the brush'. – David M Weinberg, Jerusalem Post, May 2021

'People in Gaza are living under constant attacks and pressure in an open-air prison,' - David Cameron, UK Prime Minister, 2010.

Genocide

Genocide is considered the gravest of all atrocity crimes. The UN Genocide Convention was created in 1951, as a response to the genocide committed against the Jews in Nazi Germany. According to the Convention, genocide includes the following acts committed with intent to destroy, in whole or in part, a national, ethnical, racial or religious group:

(a) Killing members of the group;

(b) Causing serious bodily or mental harm to members of the group;

(c) Deliberately inflicting on the group conditions of life calculated to bring about its physical destruction in whole or in part.

In December 2023, South Africa brought a case against Israel to the International Court of Justice under the Genocide Convention. The court found that there was a plausible case that genocide was being committed in Gaza, and the case will be heard in full in the course of time.

All state signatories to the convention are under a duty to prevent genocide where there is a risk that it may be occurring. Actions which can be taken include arms embargoes and trade and diplomatic sanctions. A small number of states have ceased weapons sales to Israel, but as of June 2024, most have ignored the duty to prevent.

Many statements made by Israeli politicians have been said to imply genocidal intent.

'There are no innocent civilians in Gaza' Isaac Herzog, President, 13/10/23

Great March of Return

On March 30th 2018 a protest began in Gaza. The blockade had been in place for 13 years, and had brought about the collapse of the economy and a chronic humanitarian crisis. During that time, more than 4,400 Palestinians had been killed and thousands injured during three military assaults by Israel.

The protests, which continued every Friday for 18 months, became known as The Great March of Return, signifying the demand by refugees of the right to return to their homes. They took place along the Gaza fence, and were largely festive occasions, though skirmishes broke out and youths threw stones and

Molotov cocktails. Israeli forces responded with tear gas and live ammunition. There was a policy of shooting protesters in the legs, leading to thousands of injuries and many permanent disabilities. More than 200 Palestinians were killed. In February 2019, a UN Human Rights Council commission found that of the 489 cases of Palestinian deaths or injuries analysed, only two were possibly justified as responses to danger by Israeli forces.

There was hope that a prolonged peaceful protest would bring about sympathy for the Palestinian cause , but initial interest from the world media did not last.

Hamas

Hamas is a '...*Palestinian Islamic national liberation and resistance movement... Its goal is to liberate Palestine and confront the Zionist project*.' (Hamas: A document of General Principles and Policies, 2017)

Hamas was founded in Gaza in 1987, shortly after the start of the first Intifada*. It created a military wing, the al-Qassam Brigades, and spearheaded the more violent aspects of the second intifada*. The group is designated a terrorist organisation by Israel, the United States, European Union, Canada, Egypt and Japan. (AJ)

Hamas grew rapidly in popularity and ran parliamentary candidates in the elections of January 2006, taking 74 seats to Fatah's 45. Attempts to form a coalition government were derailed by Israeli and US interference. The US and UK have boycotted Hamas ever since. In 2007, following internal fighting with Fatah, Hamas set up its own administration in Gaza*.

Although in its revised charter of 2017 Hamas accepted, with caveats, '*the establishment of a fully sovereign and independent Palestinian state...*' it does not recognise Israel. '*Hamas does not wage a struggle against the Jews because they are Jewish but wages a struggle against the Zionists who occupy Palestine.*'

Benjamin Netanyahu supported the transfer of funds to

Hamas by Qatar. In March 2019, he said: *'Whoever opposes a Palestinian state must support delivery of funds to Gaza because maintaining separation between the PA in the West Bank and Hamas in Gaza will prevent the establishment of a Palestinian state.'*

'The Palestinian Authority is a burden. Hamas is an asset.' Bezalel Smotrich, current Israeli Finance minister, 2015

Hasbara

Hasbara is a Hebrew word which roughly translates as 'explaining'. Since its inception, the Israeli state has put huge resources into controlling the public narrative. Its tactics include positioning Israel as the victim in all conflicts, blaming Hamas for high civilian casualty rates (see Human Shields*) and conflating criticism of Israel's actions with anti-Semitism.

Hasbara tactics operate from the highest levels of diplomacy, to the social media sphere. Public representatives of foreign states and media organisations are invited to Israel and taken on selective tours. In 2005 the Israeli government launched the 'Brand Israel' campaign, to improve Israel's reputation in the cultural sphere, but attempts to gain support from high-profile Hollywood and sporting stars largely backfired.

Since October 2023, foreign journalists have been barred from entering Gaza, but the hasbara campaign has arranged for 4000 of them to visit Israel, including 824 from the US and 595 from the UK. Social media accounts are operated by all state institutions including the IDF*. Hasbara fellowships are available to students to become 'Social Media Warriors', and large numbers of operatives are employed to undermine pro-Palestine accounts.

Human Shields

It is prohibited under international law to place or manoeuvre civilians or other protected persons (such as injured combatants or prisoners of war) specifically in order to render certain areas or forces immune from military operations.

Human shields fall into three categories: 1) 'Voluntary shields', who choose to protect a military target. 2) 'Involuntary shields', who are forced or coerced to prevent attacks, and 3) Proximate shields, which are civilian groups, or civilian buildings (such as hospitals or schools) which deter attacks by their proximity to active conflict. The use of human shields is forbidden by Protocol I of the Geneva Conventions and is considered a war crime.

In the Israeli-Palestinian context, both Israeli forces and Palestinian armed groups have faced accusations of this practice from a range of sources. Palestinian armed groups are under investigation by the ICC for using Palestinians as human shields. In June 2024, footage from the West Bank shows an injured Palestinian man tied to the front of an armoured vehicle as it moves through a built-up area.

Hezbollah

Hezbollah is a political, military and social organisation based in Lebanon. It emerged out of a large Shia movement called AMAL in response to the Israeli occupation of South Lebanon. Its resistance activities (alongside other smaller leftist factions) led to the withdrawal of the Israeli army from most of the south in May 2000. By this time it had become one of Lebanon's main political forces.

Lebanon has a sectarian power-sharing structure created to ensure all religious sects in the country have representation in government.. This system has recently led to deadlock and successive attempts to form stable administrations in Lebanon have failed. This is one of several reasons for the collapse of

Lebanon's economy, where more than 40% of the population now falls below the poverty line.

Hezbollah's military is a far stronger force than Hamas, and defeated Israeli forces in Lebanon in 2006. It takes unilateral action, as it did in supporting the Assad regime in Syria. In October 2023 Hezbollah began to exchange fire with Israel, stating that it would continue until the assault on Gaza ends. As of June 2024, what began as careful tactical exchanges are being escalated dangerously by both sides.

Hezbollah is a proscribed organisation in many countries, including the US, UK, Australia, the EU and most members of the Arab League.

IDF - Israeli Defence Forces

The IDF is the fourth largest military in the world and possesses nuclear weapons. All Jewish citizens of Israel are obliged to spend between 2 and 3 years enlisted in the IDF when they reach the age of 18. They then become reservists, available for recall to active service during times of conflict.

The IDF's exercise of crowd control, gained in its occupation of the OPT* and East Jerusalem, gives it an expertise which is valued by governments engaged in repression of their own populations. Many US police departments send officers to Israel for training.

Israelis refer to the IDF as 'the most moral army in the world,' but in recent decades, numerous investigations into its conduct in the OPT* by, among others, the UN, Human Rights Watch and B'Tselem, have found evidence of war crimes. These include the unlawful targeting and killing of civilians; the deliberate exploding of white phosphorus over populated areas and the destruction of civilian structures, including schools, hospitals, markets, and humanitarian aid warehouses. Most Palestinians refer to the IDF as the 'IOF' (Israeli Occupation Forces).

International Court of Justice

The International Court of Justice was set up in 1946 to serve as the arbiter of disputes between member states of the United Nations. As well as hearing cases, the court is asked to provide advisory opinions on issues of international law. It is currently deliberating evidence given at an oral hearing in February 2024 by 49 member states of the UN, on the Legal Consequences arising from the Policies and Practices of Israel in the Occupied Palestinian Territory, including East Jerusalem. In 2004 the ICJ ruled that Israel's Separation Wall* is illegal.

It is customary for other states to 'intervene', or present evidence, on some issue particular to each case brought before the ICJ. In the case of South Africa v Israel (see Genocide Convention*), as of May 2024, Nicaragua, Libya and Colombia have filed their declarations, but many more countries have stated an intention to intervene. Ireland was the first state in the Global North to do so on the side of South Africa. They have since been joined by Belgium. The UK, the US and Germany intend to intervene on the side of Israel.

In July 2024 the ICJ delivered its advisory opinion on the occupation of the Palestinian territories. It concluded that Israel's continued presence in Palestine is unlawful and called for Israel to cease immediately all new settlement activities, and to evacuate all settlers.

International Criminal Court

The International Criminal Court (ICC) was set up in 2002 and is governed by an international treaty called the Rome Statute. The ICC investigates and brings to trial individuals charged with the gravest crimes of concern to the international community: genocide, war crimes, crimes against humanity and the crime of aggression. It has been criticised for its heavy focus on African defendants, but in 2023 an arrest warrant was issued for Vladimir Putin for overseeing the removal of children from Ukraine.

Israel is among the 41 states that are not signatories to the Rome Statute but Palestine is a signatory, and the court has ruled that it has jurisdiction over the occupied Palestinian Territories. On the 20th May 2024 applications were made by the chief prosecutor for arrest warrants against 3 Hamas leaders (Yahya Sinwar, Mohammed Diab Ibrahim al-Masri and Ismail Haniye), with 8 charges including murder, extermination and taking hostages, and 2 Israeli leaders, (Benjamin Netanyahu and Yoav Gallant), on 7 charges, including starvation* of civilians as a method of warfare as a war crime, intentionally directing attacks against a civilian population [and] extermination and/or murder.

International Humanitarian Law (Jus in Bello)

International Humanitarian Law is the body of law dedicated to balancing military necessity with humanity in times of armed conflict, and above all protecting civilians from the consequences of war. It also provides for basic protection for combatants from superfluous suffering, mistreatment and murder. The hostilities ongoing between Israel and Palestinian armed groups are governed by IHL, which means that they may attack each others' military installations and personnel, but not civilians or civilian objects.

> '*I was the minister of justice. I am a lawyer … But I am against law – international law in particular. Law in general.*' - Tzipi Livni, Israeli Minister of Foreign Affairs, 2007

Intifada

Intifada (Arabic انتفاضة – literally 'shaking off') is generally translated as uprising. There have been two intifadas in Palestine, in resistance to Israel's occupation

First Intifada 1987 – 1993

The first intifada was sparked when an Israeli forces vehicle crashed into a car and killed its four Palestinian occupants. Demonstrations began in Gaza and spread to the West Bank.

Palestinians targeted patrols with rocks and Molotov cocktails. The Israeli forces responded with live ammunition, arrests, deportations and house demolitions. Yitzhak Rabin, Defence Minister at the time, directed the security forces to *'break their bones'*, and many protestors were permanently disabled by this policy.

The leadership of the intifada was drawn from various political and civil factions and was largely outside the influence of the PLO.* Decentralised committees provided social support as a civil disobedience movement arose, with tax strikes, withdrawal of labour and boycotting of Israeli goods. As more and more men were arrested or deported, women took on a central organisational role.

1436 Palestinians were killed during the first intifada and 421 Israelis, of which 150 were members of the security services. In addition, 489 Palestinians were deported, in breach of international law.

The first Intifada ended upon the signing of the first of the Oslo Accords* in 1993.

'This style [breaking demonstrators' bones] is far more efficient than arrestment, for an arrested person would spend 18 days in a prison… and then he would go out on the streets throwing stones and demonstrating; whereas, if the soldiers broke both his hands, then he won't be able to go on the streets

[for] at least one and a half month afterwards.' –
Yitzhak Rabin. The'Jerusalem Post, January 1988

2. Second Intifada 2000 – 2005

Following the failed promise of the Oslo Accords* and the expansion of Israeli settlements in the West Bank,* the second intifada was sparked by a provocative visit by Ariel Sharon to the Al-Aqsa Mosque in Jerusalem. Protests were violently repressed by the security forces from the start, and the peaceful elements of the first intifada were subsumed by increased militarisation and suicide bombings. Hamas* emerged as a resistance force during this time and increased in popularity, while the PLO* came to be seen as corrupt and ineffective, having no power to prevent Israeli expansion.

During this time, Sharon became Prime Minister. He reoccupied areas in the West Bank previously administered by the PA* and began construction of the Separation Wall.*

There were 138 suicide attacks and 1,038 Israelis killed between September 28, 2000 and February 8, 2005, and 3,189 Palestinians killed. In addition, 4,100 Palestinian homes were demolished and some 6,000 Palestinians arrested.

International sympathy for the Palestinian cause which had arisen in response to Israel's heavy-handed approach to the first intifada, waned again during the second Intifada.

Iron Dome

The Iron Dome is an air defence system developed by Israel that detects incoming rockets and intercepts them. It is one of the most effective air defence systems in operation, with a 90% success rate. Iron Dome batteries are deployed in all the most highly populated areas in Israel.

Israeli weapons development

'In every war against Gaza a range of weapons and surveillance tech has been deployed against the Palestinians which is then marketed and sold to huge amounts of nations around the world,' - Antony Loewenstein, author of *The Palestine Laboratory*.

Israel is the world's twelfth largest exporter of arms and is a global leader in the development of surveillance technology. In 2023 Israel's International Defence Cooperation Directorate figures showed arms and cyber-technology exports totalled $13 billion, representing a near doubling of trade in 5 years. The Asia-Pacific region accounted for 48% of weapons sales, Europe for 35%, the US 9%. The United Arab Emirates, Bahrain, and Morocco, which normalised relations with Israel in the 2020 Abraham Accords, accounted for 3% of arms purchases, down from 24% in 2022.

'You should always realise in the wars Israel had we had a dip in the economy but immediately after we had a huge spike back of innovation. And the knowledge and the experience Israel is gathering in this round of violence is second to none,' Nir Barkat, Israeli Economy Minister, to reporters in the UK, February 2024.

Jerusalem

Jerusalem (al Quds) is an ancient city of religious significance to Islam, Christianity and Judaism. The UN partition plan of 1947 called for an independent Jewish State, an independent Arab state, with Jerusalem (and Bethlehem) under separate, international administration. In the war of 1948, Jerusalem was divided, with West Jerusalem under Israeli control and East Jerusalem under Jordanian control. In the war of 1967, Israel annexed East Jerusalem.

Israeli settlements have spread into traditional Palestinian neighbourhoods, and evictions are widespread and ongoing. Palestinian residents are required to prove that they are permanently resident in the city in order to keep their permits to live there.

The two-state solution,* supported by the PA and large sections of the international community, sees East Jerusalem as the capital of a Palestinian state. In 2017, Donald Trump declared that Jerusalem was the capital of Israel and announced plans to move the US embassy there from Tel Aviv, which was actualised in May 2018. For Palestinians the move was seen as a deliberate undermining of the peace process. Mahmoud Abbas, head of the PA, said the US was 'abdicating its role as a peace mediator', and that Jerusalem is the 'eternal capital of the state of Palestine'.

Knesset

The Knesset is the single chamber legislature of Israel and is based in Tel Aviv. The Knesset passes all laws and elects the president and prime minister. It approves the cabinet and supervises the work of the government, among other things. There are 120 members, elected through proportional representation.

The government (June 2024) is a coalition of the populist Likud party and a number of far-right religious Zionist parties. The opposition is led by Yesh Atid, a centrist secular Zionist party. There are 10 Arab members in the current Knesset.

Lavender

Lavender is an artificial intelligence system used by the Israelis during the 2023/24 assault on Gaza to identify targets for air strikes. It is 'trained' using data from known members of Hamas or Palestinian Islamic Jihad and 'learns' to identify more by the application of common markers or personal connections. It draws upon the vast amount of data collected by Shin Bet, which includes facial recognition and phone monitoring.

For an article by the Israeli online journal +972, 6 anonymous members of the Israeli security forces who have worked with the Lavender system were interviewed. They testified that, although decisions by Lavender were subject to verification by human operatives, *'the emphasis was to create as many targets as possible, as quickly as possible'*. The only check they were able to implement within the few seconds allowed for each case before a strike was carried out, was whether the target was male or female. According to four of the sources, Lavender has marked some 37,000 Palestinians as suspected Hamas militants, most of them junior, for assassination.

'They wanted to allow us to attack [the suspected junior operatives] automatically. That's the Holy Grail. Once you go automatic, target generation goes crazy.'

Mossad

Mossad is the national intelligence agency of the Israeli state. and was formed soon after Israel's declaration of independence. It is one of the main entities in the Israeli Intelligence Community, along with Aman (military intelligence), and Shin Bet (internal security). Mossad is responsible for intelligence collection, covert operations, and counter-terrorism. Its director answers directly and only to the Prime Minister.

Mossad is one of the world's largest espionage agencies with an estimated annual budget of around €2.52 billion. It has a broad remit, with operatives in many parts of the world.

A 2024 investigation revealed attempts by Mossad in 2021 to deter the Chief Prosecutor of the ICC* from investigating Israeli war crimes. Mossad has also been implicated in assassinations of Palestinian and Iranian individuals in the Arab World and elsewhere.

. . .

Nakba

For Palestinians, the Nakba, ('catastrophe' in Arabic), refers to the violent displacement and dispossession of an estimated 750,000 Palestinians by Zionist militia and the newly formed Israeli army, before and during the 1948-49 Arab-Israeli war. The term is also used to encompass the ongoing violence, dispossession and land acquisition by Israel, and the denial of the right of return.*

Prior to the Nakba, Palestine was a multi-ethnic and multi-cultural society. Following the declaration of the State of Israel in 1948, Zionist forces struck out against Palestinian villages, and the conflict quickly escalated into war with the involvement of neighbouring Arab armies.

Overall, Zionist forces took more than 78% percent of historic Palestine, and ethnically cleansed and destroyed or repopulated approximately 530 villages, towns and cities. Over half the Palestinian population was permanently displaced and an estimated 15,000 Palestinians were killed in massacres and other atrocities. Following the war, the homes of displaced Palestinians were given to Jewish settlers. Today, the descendants of many of those who were forced to flee their homes in 1948 remain displaced, within Palestine and in neighbouring Arab states.

Palestinians commemorate the Nakba on the 15th May, one day after Israels' Independence Day.

Nakba Denial

Denial of the Nakba, like denial of Palestinian identity, is prevalent in Israel, erasing the record of massacres and atrocities, and claiming that Palestinians left their homes voluntarily. Within Israel this has been challenged by peace groups and by the work of New Historians working with documents declassified from the 1980s onwards.

In 2011, an amendment nicknamed the 'Nakba Law' was introduced, authorising the Israeli Minister of Finance to deny funding to any organisation or entity if it commemorates the establishment of the state of Israel as a day of mourning.

'The term 'Nakba,' originally coined to describe the magnitude of the self-inflicted Palestinian and Arab defeat in the 1948 war, has become in recent decades a synonym for Palestinian victimhood, with failed aggressors transformed into hapless victims and vice versa. Israel should do its utmost to uproot this false image by exposing its patently false historical basis.' - Dr. Raphael G. Bouchnik-Chen, retired colonel and former senior analyst in IDF Military Intelligence.

Negroponte Doctrine

On July 26, 2002, John Negroponte, the United States Ambassador to the UN, said that the United States will oppose Security Council resolutions concerning the Israeli-Palestinian conflict that condemn Israel without also condemning terrorist groups. During the assault on Gaza which began in October 2023, the US followed the Negroponte doctrine and used its veto in successive Ceasefire resolutions of the UN Security Council. It has also vetoed resolutions which include specific condemnation of Hamas.*

Normalisation

Normalisation is the term used for agreements made between Israel and Arab and majority-Muslim states. Israel was not recognised by the Arab world at its inception, and the subsequent decades have seen continual efforts by the US and Israel to enter into peace and trade agreements. Egypt and Jordan, immediate neighbours of Israel, entered peace agreements in 1979 and 1994 respectively, and the Abraham Accords, initiated by Trump in 2018, resulted in normalisation agreements in 2020 between Israel and the UAE, Morocco, Bahrain and Sudan. These agreements do not reflect the majority views in these states, and are the cause of much dissatisfaction with their leaderships.

The agreement with the UAE contains a commitment *'to realise a negotiated solution to the Israeli-Palestinian conflict'* but Israel's continued expansion of settlements and rejection of a two-state-solution suggest that the needs of the Palestinians have been side-lined by the accords, leading to high levels of resentment among the Palestinian population.

Negotiations with Saudi Arabia, which were close to finalisation in 2023, were implicated as a trigger for the October 7th attack led by Hamas. In December 2023 a survey by the pro-Israel Washington Institute for Near East Policy found that 96% of Saudis said Arab countries should break all contacts with Israel to protest against Israeli attacks in Gaza, but as of June 2024 reports suggest Saudi Arabia is again close to finalising a normalisation agreement.

Occupation

Article 42 of the 1907 Hague Regulations (HR) states that a *'territory is considered occupied when it is actually placed under the authority of the hostile army.'* Israel's occupation of Palestinian territory is the longest in modern history, and its settlement programme in the West Bank* is in contravention of the Fourth Geneva Convention (see Settlements*).

Israel maintains that it ceased to occupy Gaza* in 2005, but this is in dispute. The position of the US is unclear, but in January 2024, in response to a case brought by Al-Haq, the UK government stated that *'As a matter of treaty law, the UK's position is that Israel continues to have obligations as an Occupying Power in Gaza under Geneva Convention IV.'*

According to the convention, these obligations include: *'To the fullest extent of the means available to it, the occupying power must ensure sufficient hygiene and public health standards, as well as the provision of food and medical care to the population under occupation.'*

> *'I have ordered a complete siege on the Gaza Strip. There will be no electricity, no food, no fuel, everything is closed.' 'We are fighting human animals and we are acting accordingly'* - Yoav Gallant, Minister of defence, 09/10/2023

Occupied Palestinian Territories - OPT

This is the name used by the UN for Palestinian land under Israeli occupation, and includes Gaza, the West Bank and East Jerusalem.

One-State Solution

The idea of a single state to encompass all of Mandate Palestine has been around since the 1920s. Proponents of the idea see this state as being democratic and secular, with no religious group privileged over another.

The one state solution was proposed by several Arab states prior to the 1947 Partition Plan and is still seen by a minority of Palestinians and Israelis as the only equitable solution. It was a founding principle of the PLO* but has been replaced since the Oslo Accords* by a firm commitment to the two-state solution.*

Benjamin Netanyahu's display in the UNGA in 2023 of a map which showed no Palestinian territories confirms the intentions of his administration to deny the possibility of a Palestinian state. By its nature, Zionism requires a majority Jewish population and precludes the possibility of democratic Palestinian participation in a single, secular state. What currently exists in the region is a de facto single, apartheid* state. As of 2024, Netanyahu and his coalition government are determined to maintain its status as such.

'I will not compromise on full Israeli security control over all the territory west of Jordan - and this is contrary to a Palestinian state,' - Benjamin Netanyahu

Oil and gas

In the second half of the twentieth century, the US became the dominant player in the oil market. The price of oil is tied to the US dollar and the circulation of petrodollars is central to the global dominance of the currency. Israel is critical to the maintenance of US influence in the area.

Arab states, owners of the largest reserves of oil in the world, have become economically, politically and militarily associated with the US, and a number of free-trade agreements strengthening these ties are based upon normalisation* with Israel.

Oil and natural gas finds off the coast of Gaza are valued at $524bn. A $1.4bn project involving the Palestinian Authority, Egypt, Israel and Hamas was planned to launch gas production by March 2024. Instead, on 29 October, three weeks into its assault on Gaza, Netanyahu's government awarded 12 licences to six companies, including British Petroleum and Italy's ENI, for natural gas exploration in the Mediterranean Basin area. The appropriation of resources by an occupying power is in violation of the Hague Regulations and the Fourth Geneva Convention.

'Israel is the largest American aircraft carrier in the world that cannot be sunk, does not carry even one American soldier, and is located in a critical region for American national security.' - Alexander M. Haig, Secretary of State under Richard Nixon, 1982

Oslo Accords

The Oslo Accords resulted from secret negotiations which took place between the PLO* and the Israelis in Norway. The first Accord, signed in 1993, delivered the principles of the agreement, which provided for an interim Palestinian Authority* to have, for 5 years, a limited administrative and security role in the OPT (see West Bank*) as a means of preparing for Palestinian self-determination. The second Accord, signed in 1995, concretised the principles. The Accords imply a pathway to Palestinian statehood, though the word 'state' does not appear in any of the documents.

Among other breaches of the Accords, Israel has continued to expand settlements throughout the West Bank and their forces regularly operate in PA-administered areas, including the cities of Nablus and Ramallah.

Edward Said called the Oslo Accords *'an instrument of Palestinian surrender, a Palestinian Versailles'*. Nearly 30 years after the signing of Oslo II, the PA is still in existence and no progress has been made on the promise of a Palestinian state.

Palestinian Authority (PA)

The Palestinian Authority is the governing body established in 1994 following the Oslo Accords*. It is tasked with administering parts of the West Bank, managing civil and security affairs in these areas under limited self-governance. The PA has faced significant challenges along with a range of criticisms, not least from Palestinians themselves, for corruption and lack of democracy.

Although the PA has the appearance of a state, with ministries and a civil service, Israel maintains overall control, managing tax revenue, restricting the free movement of Palestinians and their ability to buy land or to build or extend houses in Area C. The PA is seen by many as a tool of the Israeli state. Its forces, trained by the US, keep tight control over the population, arresting not only those suspected of militant activity, but also union leaders, journalists and other critics. It is deeply unpopular. In a March 2023 survey taken by the Palestinian Centre for Policy and Survey Research, 63% of West Bank residents stated that they considered the PA a burden on the people.

In the elections of 2005, Mahmoud Abbas was voted President of the PA for a four year term. However, no further elections have been held and Abbas remains President, amidst accusations of corruption and links to violence. US stated policy is for the PA to take control in whatever is left of Gaza following a ceasefire, but as of June 2024, the Israeli government is opposed to the plan.

PLO

The Palestine Liberation Organisation (PLO) came into being in 1964, as an umbrella for several Palestinian resistance organisations. Yasser Arafat became chairman in 1969. Starting in the late 1960s, the PLO launched attacks on Israel from its bases in Jordan. In 1971, following the Popular Front for the Liberation of Palestine (PFLP) hijackings of 5 civilian aircraft, the PLO was forced to relocate from Jordan, shifting its headquarters to Lebanon.

There were further attacks outside Israel, including the Black September murders at the Munich Olympics, but in 1974 Arafat called for an end to them and the PLO confined itself to a military campaign against Israel. This resulted in Israel's invasion of Lebanon and the siege of Beirut in 1982.

In 1988, the PLO declared the establishment of the State of Palestine, and has since been internationally recognised as the representative of the Palestinian people. The PLO is the holder of the Palestinian seat in the UN, not the Palestinian Authority.*

Proportionality

Proportionality is a principle of International Humanitarian Law which dictates that attacks on military objectives are unlawful if the incidental civilian harm expected is disproportionate to the overall military advantage anticipated. Israel has long been accused of launching disproportionate attacks, and such attacks were the subject of an investigation by the International Criminal Court before October 7th.

In the weeks and months following October 7th 2023, directives given to Israeli operatives were that 15 or 20 civilian deaths would be acceptable when targeting a suspected junior member of Hamas. Those identified as such by Lavender* were assassinated with dumb bombs. These bombs, unlike the more expensive and 'surgical' smart bombs, collapse buildings and kill everyone inside them. In many cases Israeli air strikes wiped out entire families, including people in the same building who had no relationship to the primary target.

For a strike against a senior Hamas operative, 100 or even more civilian casualties was considered acceptable.

Israeli forces have killed civilians in schools, hospitals and places of worship, while fleeing to 'safe' areas, and while looking for food and water. Figures given by the United Nations in April 2024 show that, out of the 34000+ Palestinians killed, more than two-thirds were women and children.

Recognition of Palestine

On 22nd May 2024, Ireland, Norway and Spain joined 143 other members of the UN in formally recognising the State of Palestine. Recognition of Palestine is symbolic, and supposes the eventual implementation of a two-state-solution.* Slovenia joined them on the 5th June, meaning that 147 of the 193 member states of the UN now recognise Palestine. The extent of the territory referred to as 'Palestine' is not specified in statements of recognition.

Interpretation of the meaning of such gestures is divided. *'We had hoped to recognise Palestine as part of a two-state peace deal but instead we recognise Palestine to keep the hope of that two-state solution alive.'* - Ireland's Taoiseach, Simon Harris, 22nd May 2024.

But the majority opinion among scholars and academics, according to Tamar Megiddo, a senior lecturer at Hebrew University's Department of International Relations, is that *'Palestine is in fact already a state – these countries are merely acknowledging this to be true.'*

(See also United Nations - Palestine)

Refugees

The 1951 Refugee Convention defines a refugee as a person who 'owing to well-founded fear of being persecuted for reasons of race, religion, nationality, membership of a particular social group or political opinion, is outside the country of [their] nationality and is unable or, owing to such fear, is unwilling to avail [themself] of the protection of that country.' (UNHCR, the UN Refugee Agency.)

UNHCR protects around 37.5 million refugees, but a further 6 million Palestine refugees are supported under a separate mandate (see UNRWA.*)

Refugee Camps

Camps are areas in which refugees established themselves in the aftermath of the Nakba*. They began as tent camps, but are now built-up urban areas. There are Palestinian refugee camps in occupied Palestine and others in Lebanon, Jordan and Syria. Those outside Palestine retain a strong Palestinian identity and people are still known by reference to the village they were expelled from, often living in groupings that match their original villages.

Resistance to Occupation

In 1982, United Nations General Assembly Resolution 37/43 affirmed *'the legitimacy of the struggle for independence, territorial integrity, national unity, and liberation from foreign domination and foreign occupation by all available means, including armed struggle.'* This resolution openly recognised the right to use force against foreign illegal occupation, which it considers a serious threat to international peace and security, and specifically recalled the cases of Namibia and Palestine.

Such use of force is governed by International Humanitarian Law, which calls for distinction to be made between civilians and combatants and between civilian objects and military objectives..

Return

1. Right of Return

One of the core principles set out in the Universal Declaration of Human Rights is the right of return. Article 13(b) of the UDHR states: *'Everyone has the right to leave any country, including his own, and to return to his country.'*

In addition, UN General Assembly Resolution 194, passed in 1948 and referring to Palestine, states that *'the refugees wishing to return to their homes and live at peace with their neighbours should be permitted to do so at the earliest practicable date...'* Israel's admission as a member of the UN was made conditional on its acceptance and implementation of resolutions including UN Resolution 194. Many subsequent UN resolutions have validated the Palestinians' right of return. Israel has consistently refused to allow Palestinians to return.

The Oslo Accords* undermined the right of return by accepting the premise of a two-state solution, which would make it impossible for refugees to return to their place of origin within Israel.

Israel believes that UNRWA* is responsible for the right of return being extended to the descendants of refugees, but this right is also evidenced in international law and recognised by the UN High Commission for Refugees.

2.Law of Return

The Law of Return, passed in the Israeli Knesset* in July 1950, states that *'Every Jew has the right to come to this country as an oleh* (immigrant to Israel). Organisations such as Nefesh B'Nefesh and The Jewish Agency for Israel assist Jewish immigrants with documentation and free flights. New immigrants receive Israeli citizenship and are helped to find jobs and accommodation.

The process of becoming an Israeli citizen is known as 'Aliyah' (Hebrew, lit. *ascent*). Since 1948 more than 3 million Jews have made aliyah. Many olehs find homes in the expanding settlements, but there are documented cases of Palestinians being removed from their houses to make them available to new arrivals from the USA or Europe.

Self-defence

Israel and its supporters around the world justify its assaults on Gaza as self-defence. However, under international law, the right to self-defence does not extend to an occupying power waging war on the people under its occupation.

Self-determination

Self-determination is the right of a people to form its own political entity. Throughout the twentieth century many nations freed themselves from colonial rule and declared independence under this right.

Under international law, Palestinians have the right to self-determination, but since its inception, Israel has prevented them from exercising this right.

Resolution 52/34, adopted by the UN Human Rights Council on 4 April 2023:

1. Reaffirms the inalienable, permanent and unqualified right of the Palestinian people to self-determination, including their right to live in freedom, justice and dignity and the right to their independent State of Palestine;

3. Calls upon Israel, the occupying Power, to immediately end its occupation of the Occupied Palestinian Territory, including East Jerusalem, and to reverse and redress any impediments to the political independence, sovereignty and territorial integrity of Palestine, and reaffirms its support for the solution of two States, Palestine and Israel, living side by side in peace and security.

Separation Wall / Separation Barrier

Construction of the Separation Wall by Israel began in 2002 at the height of the second Intifada, ostensibly for security purposes.

When fully complete the barrier will be 713 km long and engulf almost 10% of the West Bank. The route of the wall constitutes a de facto redrawing of the 1949 Armistice Line (Green Line). The current and projected route runs only partly along the Green Line, with the vast majority (85%) encroaching well into Palestinian land in the West Bank, disrupting Palestinian communities, preventing access to farmlands, education and employment, restricting freedom of movement, and impeding or blocking access to resources and vital services. In 2004 the International Court of Justice* ruled that the wall's construction on occupied territory is contrary to international law. Despite this, construction continued and the wall remains. Displays of art, graffiti, and pro-liberation murals regularly appear on the Palestinian side of the wall.

Further encroachment upon Palestinian land in the West Bank* has occurred with Israel's creation of so-called 'seam zones', designated as closed military areas, between the Wall and the Green Line. The building of illegal settlements has been encouraged within these areas. As of 2022 the UN estimates that 50,000 Palestinians, across 57 communities, live within seam zones, suffering displacement, loss of land and livelihoods, separation from family, and severe restriction of movement.

Settlements

Under International law, Israeli settlements in the Occupied Palestinian Territories are illegal. Article 49 of the Fourth Geneva Convention states that: *'Collective or individual forcible transfers of population from and within the occupied territory are prohibited'* and *'Transfers of the civilian population of the occupying power into the occupied territory, regardless whether forcible or voluntary, are prohibited'.*

There are approximately 250 Israeli settlements in the Occupied West Bank, connected to each other and to major conurbations by a network of roads, many of which are prohibited for Palestinians (see Apartheid*). In February 2023 a report by WestBankJewishPopulationStats.com stated the settler population had grown to 502,991. These figures do not include approximately 200,000 settlers in East Jerusalem and the Occupied Golan Heights.

In February 2024 Finance Minister Bezalel Smotrich announced plans for 3,426 new Israeli homes to be built in the West Bank, making a record 18,515 homes which have been approved in the West Bank over the year and two months since the Netanyahu government took power. In July Israel approved the biggest seizure of Palestinian land in three decades, declaring 12.7 square km in the Jordan Valley to be 'state property'.

Settler Violence

Settler violence is an ongoing threat to Palestinians living in the West Bank and East Jerusalem. Campaigns of harassment are continual in both rural and urban areas. In 2021 the OHCHR

(UN Human Rights Council) reported an increase in settler violence, with more than 400 incidents recorded. *The Israeli Government and its military have done far too little to curb this violence and to protect the Palestinians under siege. In several cases, Israeli security forces and outsourced private security companies stand by and take no action to prevent the violence; instead, they respond to settler-related violence by ordering Palestinians to leave the area, including Palestinian-owned land, or even actively support the settlers.'*

2023 was the worst year on record for settler violence, even before the events of October 7th. Since that day the violence has spiked and the distinction between settlers and Israeli forces has become increasingly blurred. The UN Office for the Coordination of Humanitarian Affairs recorded 1,096 settler attacks on Palestinians in the territory between October 7 and March 31. Israeli forces and settlers killed more than 500 Palestinians in the West Bank between October 2023 and June 2024.

Settler-colonialism

Classical colonialism is based upon the oppression of indigenous people. Their resources and labour are exploited for the benefit of the colonisers, who remain distinct and separate. Settler-colonialism is the process whereby indigenous populations are supplanted by the colonial power. Examples of settler-colonial societies include North America, Australia and Israel. In all these cases, indigenous people have been massacred or displaced in order to clear the land for the use of the coloniser. While some dispossessed people may continue to live in the settler state, they do so under conditions decided by the colonisers, and have no rights, or restricted rights, to the use of their land. In some cases, reservations are created for the indigenous population, with or without limited degrees of self-determination.

Settler-colonialism is often carried out under the claim that the land is empty. Australia was considered *'Terra Nullius'*

(Latin, - the land of no one) by early settlers. In Israel the concept of '*A land without a people for a people without a land*' was a core Zionist principle.

In Palestine, the settler-colonialist project continues to expand, with regular 'acquisitions' of Palestinian land in the West Bank, and evictions of Palestinians from their homes.

> *'I do not agree that the dog in a manger has the final right to the manger even though he may have lain there for a very long time. I do not admit that right. I do not admit for instance, that a great wrong has been done to the Red Indians of America or the black people of Australia. I do not admit that a wrong has been done to these people by the fact that a stronger race, a higher-grade race, a more worldly wise race to put it that way, has come in and taken their place.'* – Winston Churchill, to the Palestine Royal Commission, 1937.

Starvation

Starvation as a weapon of war is prohibited under international law. In the wake of the 7th October attacks in 2023 Israel blocked the supply of food, medicine, and essential aid to civilians in Gaza, whilst subjecting the area to aerial bombardment and a ground offensive. This led rapidly to widespread malnutrition, and a related rise in child mortality rates. While Israel argues that the blockade is necessary to restrict the flow of weapons to Hamas, the ICJ,* as well as Palestinian and international human rights organisations contend that the siege constitutes a form of collective punishment, placing the population at risk of famine. In March 2024, a UN-coordinated report estimated that 70% of the population in Northern Gaza was experiencing catastrophic hunger. Following months of blockade and bombardment, a UNICEF report (6th June 2024) stated that nine out of 10 children in Gaza are suffering from severe food poverty.

Starvation is included in the crimes for which, in May 2024, the ICC chief prosecutor applied for arrest warrants for two Israeli Knesset members.

Two-state solution

The two-state solution proposes the creation of an independent State of Palestine alongside the State of Israel. The version of this state currently supported by the PA* and large parts of the International Community is based upon the 1967 borders, before Israel occupied the West Bank and Gaza, with East Jerusalem as its capital. These borders would give Palestinians self-determination in 22% of Mandate Palestine.

United Nations – Israeli membership.

The State of Israel owes its existence as a legal entity to Resolution 181 of the United Nations (the UN Partition Plan) which was passed in November 1947. Since its acceptance as a member in 1949, Israel has had a troubled relationship with the United Nations. Successive resolutions of the Security Council relating to the expansion of illegal settlements and human rights abuses of Palestinians have been vetoed by the US under the Negroponte Doctrine.* Of those resolutions that have passed, whether in the General Assembly or the Security Council, most have been ignored by Israel, as has a legal opinion handed down by the ICJ* and countless reports by human rights bodies operating under the auspices of the UN.

In May 2024, in response to a vote extending the rights and privileges of Palestinian membership* of the UN, Gilad Erdan, the Israeli ambassador, accused the UN of opening itself to '*modern day Nazis*' and shredded a copy of the United Nations

Charter. In a radio interview, he called the UN a *'terror organ-isation'*.

> **'From the perspective of the UN, Israel has repeat-edly flouted fundamental UN tenets.'** - report from the United Nations Association (UK) in 2004.

United Nations - Palestinian membership.

In 2012 the status of the PLO* at the UN was upgraded to that of a Permanent Observer State under the name Palestine. Observer status allows it to participate in all of the organisation's proceedings, except for voting on draft resolutions and decisions in its main organs and bodies, from the Security Council to the General Assembly and its six main committees.

On May 10th 2024 Palestine's status was again upgraded by a Resolution of the General Assembly. New rights, to come into effect in September 2024, include: To be seated among Member States in alphabetical order, to submit proposals and amend-ments, and the right of members of the delegation of the State of Palestine to be elected as officers in the plenary and the Main Committees of the General Assembly. The General Assembly cannot make decisions on membership, but the resolution also *'determines that the State of Palestine ... should therefore be admitted to membership'* and it *'recommends that the Security Council reconsider the matter favourably'*.

UNRWA - The United Nations Relief and Works Agency

UNRWA was established in 1949 by the UN General Assembly to provide relief to refugees of the 1948 Nakba*. Subsequent waves of refugees come under its remit, as do their descendants. It is separate from the UN High Commission for

Refugees, which supports refugees from other parts of the world. Unlike the UNHCR, it is dependent on voluntary contributions from member states.

UNRWA supports Palestinian refugees in the West Bank and Gaza, Lebanon, Syria and Jordan. It provides education, healthcare, relief and social services, camp infrastructure and emergency assistance. It has a staff of 30,000. More than 5.6 million Palestinians are registered with UNRWA.

Israel wants to see UNRWA defunded and responsibilities for Palestinian refugees transferred to the UNHCR, (see Right of Return*). In January 2024 Israel accused 12 UNRWA employees of participating in the October 7th attacks. In response, many major state donors ceased funding to UNRWA. By June 2024, with the Israeli accusations still unsubstantiated, most had resumed funding.

As of June 2024, Israeli forces have killed 273 aid workers, most of them UNRWA employees, during the most recent assault on Gaza.

US/Israel relations

The Arab world holds vast oil and gas reserves. The US maintains control of its interests in the region through economic, diplomatic and military means. Its motivation is set out by the US Security Council in the 'Wolfowitz Doctrine' of 1992.

'[*The United States'*] *goal is to preclude any hostile power from dominating a region critical to our interests... These regions include Europe, East Asia, the Middle East/Persian Gulf, and Latin America.*'

Iran remains the biggest foreign policy challenge to the US in the region. It backs Hamas and Hezbollah as well as the Houthis in Yemen, though they all operate independently and not under orders from Iran.

Israel has always been central to US aims in the area. '*Were there not an Israel, the United States of America would have to invent an Israel, to protect our interests in the region.'* Joe Biden, June 5 1986. He repeated this sentiment on October 18 2023 - '*If Israel didn't exist we'd have to invent it.'*

US involvement in Israel's policies is not confined to the supply of funds and weapons. Invasion of the Gaza strip has been anticipated since Hamas took power there in 2006. '*What they really want is the forceful takeover of the territory by a bolstered Palestinian Authority. Senior officers of the American army are going back and forth between Washington, Ramallah and Jerusalem, in an effort to draw a picture of the reality on the ground... A broad Israeli operation, with American encouragement, will be able to begin only after the forces of Abbas are trained.'* - Haaretz, 2008.

War crimes

War crimes are all criminal violations of International Humanitarian Law.

The West Bank

The West Bank covers 5,650-square-km. Israelis call it by its Biblical name, Judaea and Samaria, and claim it to be part of Israel. It was under Jordanian administration until 1967 when, following the Six-Day-War, it was occupied by Israel.

Under the Oslo Accords* in 1993 the West Bank was divided into 3 administrative areas – A, B and C. Area C is described as a 'military zone' and the PA* has no administrative or security function there. It has the smallest Palestinian population of the three areas and contains the majority of Israeli settlements. A time schedule for the handover of Area C to the control of the PA was never honoured. More than 400,000 settlers now live in Area C, in what amounts to a de facto annexation.

Settlement* expansion and appropriation of Palestinian homes and land by way of quasi-legal instruments continues.

Small outposts appear regularly in rural districts and their occupants graze stock on land owned by Palestinian farmers. Objections are largely ignored, and if conflicts arise the authorities usually support the settlers.

Where's Daddy?

Where's Daddy describes a system which alerts Israeli forces to the arrival at their home of a target identified by Lavender.* *'We were not interested in killing [Hamas] operatives only when they were in a military building or engaged in a military activity,'* an intelligence officer said. *'On the contrary, the IDF bombed them in homes without hesitation, as a first option. It's much easier to bomb a family's home. The system is built to look for them in these situations.'* – unidentified intelligence officer interviewed by Israeli magazine +972. *'In the majority of cases military activity is not conducted from these targeted homes.'*

> *'Israel monitors every little step in the Gaza Strip. Every SIM card in the Gaza Strip is monitored. A lot of times when they say they're targeting a person, they're targeting the SIM card. So, what we have is a whole massive apparatus of surveillance that has existed for years for military use.'* – Neve Gordon, professor of international law and human rights at Queen Mary University of London, interviewed on Democracy Now.

Zionism

Zionism is the expression of a desire within elements of the Jewish diaspora to establish a Jewish national homeland in Palestine. It became a movement in Eastern Europe in the late 19th Century, spearheaded by Austrian journalist, Theodor

Herzl, whose pamphlet, 'The Jewish State' became a founding document of the movement. Zionism was given political legitimacy by the Balfour Declaration* in 1917. With the declaration of Independence by Israel in 1948, the movement's aspirations were actualised.

Modern political Zionism is focused on the existence of a State; it is to be distinguished from other expressions of Jewish belonging and connection to their holy land, which were respected by Christians and Muslims in Palestine before the emergence of Zionism.

Zionist principles determine that Israel remains a majority Jewish state. Immigration to Israel is confined to people of Jewish origin. Within Zionism there is a range of views: some believe in the possibility of a two-state solution*, others aspire to the creation of 'Greater Israel', an area which includes all of modern Palestine, along with parts of Lebanon, Syria, Jordan and Egypt.

FURTHER READING

Books

The Palestine Laboratory – Anthony Loewenstein

The Hundred Year War on Palestine – Rashid Khalili

Palestinian Walks – Raja Shehadeh

The Ethnic Cleansing of the Palestinians – Ilan Pappe

The End of the Peace Process - Oslo and After - Edward Said

Three Worlds - Avi Shlaim

The Battle for Justice in Palestine - Ali Abunimah

The Israel Lobby and US Foreign Policy, - John Mearsheimer and Stephen Wall

Links

+972 online www.972mag.com

www.aljazeera.com

www.electronicintifada.net

www.bdsmovement.net

https://decolonizepalestine.com/

https://www.alhaq.org/

https://www.adalah.org/

https://www.plands.org/en/home

www.visualizingpalestine.org

https://www.badil.org/

ACKNOWLEDGMENTS

Thanks to Vicky Donnelly, Dearbhla Minogue and Martin Roper for their contributions to this book. Thanks to Raja Shehadeh, Rachel Murphy, Rabie Mustapha, Ríonach Ní Néill and Niamh Keady-Tabbal for invaluable suggestions and corrections. Thanks, finally, to Sliman Mansour for permission to use his artwork on the cover.

Cover image. Olive Tree Grove, Sliman Mansour, 2012